T0144271

Ancient Ballads and Legends of Hindustan

Ancient Ballads and Legends of Hindustan

Toru Dutt

MINT EDITIONS

Ancient Ballads and Legends of Hindustan was first published in 1882.

This edition published by Mint Editions 2021.

ISBN 9781513135489 | E-ISBN 9781513212043

Published by Mint Editions®

 MINT
EDITIONS

minteditionbooks.com

Publishing Director: Jennifer Newens
Design & Production: Rachel Lopez Metzger
Project Manager: Micaela Clark
Typesetting: Westchester Publishing Services

Contents

I

SAVITRI

Part I

Savitri was the only child
    Of Madra's wise and mighty king;
Stern warriors, when they saw her, smiled,
    As mountains smile to see the spring.
Fair as a lotus when the moon
    Kisses its opening petals red,
After sweet showers in sultry June!
    With happier heart, and lighter tread,
Chance strangers, having met her, past,
    And often would they turn the head
A lingering second look to cast,
    And bless the vision ere it fled.

What was her own peculiar charm?
    The soft black eyes, the raven hair,
The curving neck, the rounded arm,
    All these are common everywhere.
Her charm was this—upon her face
    Childlike and innocent and fair,
No man with thought impure or base
    Could ever look;—the glory there,
The sweet simplicity and grace,
    Abashed the boldest; but the good
God's purity there loved to trace,
    Mirrored in dawning womanhood.

In those far-off primeval days
    Fair India's daughters were not pent
In closed zenanas. On her ways
    Savitri at her pleasure went
Whither she chose,—and hour by hour

With young companions of her age,
    She roamed the woods for fruit or flower,
        Or loitered in some hermitage,
    For to the Munis gray and old
        Her presence was as sunshine glad,
    They taught her wonders manifold
        And gave her of the best they had.

Her father let her have her way
    In all things, whether high or low;
He feared no harm; he knew no ill
    Could touch a nature pure as snow.
Long childless, as a priceless boon
    He had obtained this child at last
By prayers, made morning, night, and noon
    With many a vigil, many a fast;
Would Shiva his own gift recall,
    Or mar its perfect beauty ever?—
No, he had faith,—he gave her all
    She wished, and feared and doubted never.

And so she wandered where she pleased
    In boyish freedom. Happy time!
No small vexations ever teased,
    Nor crushing sorrows dimmed her prime.
One care alone, her father felt—
    Where should he find a fitting mate
For one so pure?—His thoughts long dwelt
    On this as with his queen he sate.
"Ah, whom, dear wife, should we select?"
    "Leave it to God," she answering cried,
"Savitri, may herself elect
    Some day, her future lord and guide."

Months passed, and lo, one summer morn
    As to the hermitage she went
Through smiling fields of waving corn,
    She saw some youths on sport intent,
Sons of the hermits, and their peers,

And one among them tall and lithe
Royal in port,—on whom the years
    Consenting, shed a grace so blithe,
So frank and noble, that the eye
    Was loth to quit that sun-browned face;
She looked and looked,—then gave a sigh,
    And slackened suddenly her pace.

What was the meaning—was it love?
    Love at first sight, as poets sing,
Is then no fiction? Heaven above
    Is witness, that the heart its king
Finds often like a lightning flash;
    We play,—we jest,—we have no care,—
When hark a step,—there comes no crash,—
    But life, or silent slow despair.
Their eyes just met,—Savitri past
    Into the friendly Muni's hut,
Her heart-rose opened had at last—
    Opened no flower can ever shut.

In converse with the gray-haired sage
    She learnt the story of the youth,
His name and place and parentage—
    Of royal race he was in truth.
Satyavan was he hight,—his sire
    Dyoumatsen had been Salva's king,
But old and blind, opponents dire
    Had gathered round him in a ring
And snatched the sceptre from his hand;
    Now,—with his queen and only son
He lived a hermit in the land,
    And gentler hermit was there none.

With many tears was said and heard
    The story,—and with praise sincere
Of Prince Satyavan; every word
    Sent up a flush on cheek and ear,
Unnoticed. Hark! The bells remind

'Tis time to go,—she went away,
    Leaving her virgin heart behind,
        And richer for the loss. A ray,
    Shot down from heaven, appeared to tinge
        All objects with supernal light,
    The thatches had a rainbow fringe,
        The cornfields looked more green and bright.

Savitri's first care was to tell
    Her mother all her feelings new;
The queen her own fears to dispel
    To the king's private chamber flew.
"Now what is it, my gentle queen,
    That makes thee hurry in this wise?"
She told him, smiles and tears between,
    All she had heard; the king with sighs
Sadly replied:—"I fear me much!
    Whence is his race and what his creed?
Not knowing aught, can we in such
    A matter delicate, proceed?"

As if the king's doubts to allay,
    Came Narad Muni to the place
A few days after. Old and gray,
    All loved to see the gossip's face,
Great Brahma's son,—adored of men,
    Long absent, doubly welcome he
Unto the monarch, hoping then
    By his assistance, clear to see.
No god in heaven, nor king on earth,
    But Narad knew his history,—
The sun's, the moon's, the planets' birth
    Was not to him a mystery.

"Now welcome, welcome, dear old friend,
    All hail, and welcome once again!"
The greeting had not reached its end,
    When glided like a music-strain
Savitri's presence through the room.—

"And who is this bright creature, say,
    Whose radiance lights the chamber's gloom—
        Is she an Apsara or fay?"
"No son thy servant hath, alas!
        This is my one,—my only child";—
"And married?"—"No."—"The seasons pass,
        Make haste, O king,"—he said, and smiled.

"That is the very theme, O sage,
    In which thy wisdom ripe I need;
Seen hath she at the hermitage
    A youth to whom in very deed
Her heart inclines."—"And who is he?"
    "My daughter, tell his name and race,
Speak as to men who best love thee."
    She turned to them her modest face,
And answered quietly and clear.—
    "Ah, no! ah, no!—It cannot be—
Choose out another husband, dear,"—
    The Muni cried,—"or woe is me!"

"And why should I? When I have given
    My heart away, though but in thought,
Can I take back? Forbid it, Heaven!
    It were a deadly sin, I wot.
And why should I? I know no crime
    In him or his."—"Believe me, child,
My reasons shall be clear in time,
    I speak not like a madman wild;
Trust me in this."—"I cannot break
    A plighted faith,—I cannot bear
A wounded conscience."—"Oh, forsake
    This fancy, hence may spring despair."—

"It may not be."—The father heard
    By turns the speakers, and in doubt
Thus interposed a gentle word,—
    "Friend should to friend his mind speak out,
Is he not worthy? tell us."—"Nay,

All worthiness is in Satyavan,
And no one can my praise gainsay:
    Of solar race—more god than man!
Great Soorasen, his ancestor,
    And Dyoumatsen his father blind
Are known to fame: I can aver
    No kings have been so good and kind."

"Then where, O Muni, is the bar?
    If wealth be gone, and kingdom lost,
His merit still remains a star,
    Nor melts his lineage like the frost.
For riches, worldly power, or rank
    I care not,—I would have my son
Pure, wise, and brave,—the Fates I thank
    I see no hindrance, no, not one."
"Since thou insistest, King, to hear
    The fatal truth,—I tell you,—I,
Upon this day as rounds the year
    The young Prince Satyavan shall die."

This was enough. The monarch knew
    The future was no sealèd book
To Brahma's son. A clammy dew
    Spread on his brow,—he gently took
Savitri's palm in his, and said:
    "No child can give away her hand,
A pledge is nought unsanctionèd;
    And here, if right I understand,
There was no pledge at all,—a thought,
    A shadow,—barely crossed the mind—
Unblamed, it may be clean forgot,
    Before the gods it cannot bind."

"And think upon the dreadful curse
    Of widowhood; the vigils, fasts,
And penances; no life is worse
    Than hopeless life,—the while it lasts.
Day follows day in one long round,

Monotonous and blank and drear;
Less painful were it to be bound
    On some bleak rock, for aye to hear—
Without one chance of getting free—
    The ocean's melancholy voice!
Mine be the sin,—if sin there be,
    But thou must make a different choice."

In the meek grace of virginhood
    Unblanched her cheek, undimmed her eye,
Savitri, like a statue, stood,
    Somewhat austere was her reply.
"Once, and once only, all submit
    To Destiny,—'tis God's command;
Once, and once only, so 'tis writ,
    Shall woman pledge her faith and hand;
Once, and once only, can a sire
    Unto his well-loved daughter say,
In presence of the witness fire,
    I give thee to this man away."

"Once, and once only, have I given
    My heart and faith—'tis past recall;
With conscience none have ever striven,
    And none may strive, without a fall.
Not the less solemn was my vow
    Because unheard, and oh! the sin
Will not be less, if I should now
    Deny the feeling felt within.
Unwedded to my dying day
    I must, my father dear, remain;
'Tis well, if so thou will'st, but say
    Can man balk Fate, or break its chain?

"If Fate so rules, that I should feel
    The miseries of a widow's life,
Can man's device the doom repeal?
    Unequal seems to be a strife,
Between Humanity and Fate;

None have on earth what they desire;
Death comes to all or soon or late;
    And peace is but a wandering fire;
Expediency leads wild astray;
    The Right must be our guiding star;
Duty our watchword, come what may;
    Judge for me, friends,—as wiser far."

She said, and meekly looked to both.
    The father, though he patient heard,
To give the sanction still seemed loth,
    But Narad Muni took the word.
"Bless thee, my child! 'Tis not for us
    To question the Almighty will,
Though cloud on cloud loom ominous,
    In gentle rain they may distil."
At this, the monarch—"Be it so!
    I sanction what my friend approves;
All praise to Him, whom praise we owe;
    My child shall wed the youth she loves."

Part II

Great joy in Madra. Blow the shell
    The marriage over to declare!
And now to forest-shades where dwell
    The hermits, wend the wedded pair.
The doors of every house are hung
    With gay festoons of leaves and flowers;
And blazing banners broad are flung,
    And trumpets blown from castle towers!
Slow the procession makes its ground
    Along the crowded city street:
And blessings in a storm of sound
    At every step the couple greet.

Past all the houses, past the wall,
    Past gardens gay, and hedgerows trim,
Past fields, where sinuous brooklets small

With molten silver to the brim
Glance in the sun's expiring light,
　　Past frowning hills, past pastures wild,
At last arises on the sight,
　　Foliage on foliage densely piled,
The woods primeval, where reside
　　The holy hermits;—henceforth here
Must live the fair and gentle bride:
　　But this thought brought with it no fear.

Fear! With her husband by her still?
　　Or weariness! Where all was new?
Hark! What a welcome from the hill!
　　There gathered are a hermits few.
Screaming the peacocks upward soar;
　　Wondering the timid wild deer gaze;
And from Briarean fig-trees hoar
　　Look down the monkeys in amaze
As the procession moves along;
　　And now behold, the bridegroom's sire
With joy comes forth amid the throng;—
　　What reverence his looks inspire!

Blind! With his partner by his side!
　　For them it was a hallowed time!
Warmly they greet the modest bride
　　With her dark eyes and front sublime!
One only grief they feel.—Shall she
　　Who dwelt in palace halls before,
Dwell in their huts beneath the tree?
　　Would not their hard life press her sore;—
The manual labour, and the want
　　Of comforts that her rank became,
Valkala robes, meals poor and scant,
　　All undermine the fragile frame?

To see the bride, the hermits' wives
　　And daughters gathered to the huts,
Women of pure and saintly lives!

And there beneath the betel-nuts
Tall trees like pillars, they admire
    Her beauty, and congratulate
The parents, that their hearts' desire
    Had thus accorded been by Fate,
And Satyavan their son had found
    In exile lone, a fitting mate:
And gossips add,—good signs abound;
    Prosperity shall on her wait.

Good signs in features, limbs, and eyes,
    That old experience can discern,
Good signs on earth and in the skies,
    That it could read at every turn.
And now with rice and gold, all bless
    The bride and bridegroom,—and they go
Happy in others' happiness,
    Each to her home, beneath the glow
Of the late risen moon that lines
    With silver, all the ghost-like trees,
Sals, tamarisks, and South-Sea pines,
    And palms whose plumes wave in the breeze.

False was the fear, the parents felt,
    Savitri liked her new life much;
Though in a lowly home she dwelt
    Her conduct as a wife was such
As to illumine all the place;
    She sickened not, nor sighed, nor pined;
But with simplicity and grace
    Discharged each household duty kind.
Strong in all manual work,—and strong
    To comfort, cherish, help, and pray,
The hours past peacefully along
    And rippling bright, day followed day.

At morn Satyavan to the wood
    Early repaired and gathered flowers
And fruits, in its wild solitude,

And fuel,—till advancing hours
Apprised him that his frugal meal
    Awaited him. Ah, happy time!
Savitri, who with fervid zeal
    Had said her orisons sublime,
And fed the Bramins and the birds,
    Now ministered. Arcadian love,
With tender smiles and honeyed words,
    All bliss of earth thou art above!

And yet there was a spectre grim,
    A skeleton in Savitri's heart,
Looming in shadow, somewhat dim,
    But which would never thence depart.
It was that fatal, fatal speech
    Of Narad Muni. As the days
Slipt smoothly past, each after each,
    In private she more fervent prays.
But there is none to share her fears,
    For how could she communicate
The sad cause of her bidden tears?
    The doom approached, the fatal date.

No help from man. Well, be it so!
    No sympathy,—it matters not!
God can avert the heavy blow!
    He answers worship. Thus she thought.
And so, her prayers, by day and night,
    Like incense rose unto the throne;
Nor did she vow neglect or rite
    The Veds enjoin or helpful own.
Upon the fourteenth of the moon,
    As nearer came the time of dread,
In Joystee, that is May or June,
    She vowed her vows and Bramins fed.

And now she counted e'en the hours,
    As to Eternity they past;
O'er head the dark cloud darker lowers,

The year is rounding full at last.
Today,—today,—with doleful sound
    The word seem'd in her ear to ring!
O breaking heart,—thy pain profound
    Thy husband knows not, nor the king,
Exiled and blind, nor yet the queen;
    But One knows in His place above.
Today,—today,—it will be seen
    Which shall be victor, Death or Love!

Incessant in her prayers from morn,
    The noon is safely tided,—then
A gleam of faint, faint hope is born,
    But the heart fluttered like a wren
That sees the shadow of the hawk
    Sail on,—and trembles in affright,
Lest a down-rushing swoop should mock
    Its fortune, and o'erwhelm it quite.
The afternoon has come and gone
    And brought no change;—should she rejoice?
The gentle evening's shades come on,
    When hark!—She hears her husband's voice!

"The twilight is most beautiful!
    Mother, to gather fruit I go,
And fuel,—for the air is cool
    Expect me in an hour or so."
"The night, my child, draws on apace,"
    The mother's voice was heard to say,
"The forest paths are hard to trace
    In darkness,—till the morrow stay."
"Not hard for me, who can discern
    The forest-paths in any hour,
Blindfold I could with ease return,
    And day has not yet lost its power."

"He goes then," thought Savitri, "thus
    With unseen bands Fate draws us on
Unto the place appointed us;

We feel no outward force,—anon
We go to marriage or to death
    At a determined time and place;
We are her playthings; with her breath
    She blows us where she lists in space.
What is my duty? It is clear,
    My husband I must follow; so,
While he collects his forest gear
    Let me permission get to go."

His sire she seeks,—the blind old king,
    And asks from him permission straight.
"My daughter, night with ebon wing
    Hovers above; the hour is late.
My son is active, brave, and strong,
    Conversant with the woods, he knows
Each path; methinks it would be wrong
    For thee to venture where he goes,
Weak and defenceless as thou art,
    At such a time. If thou wert near
Thou might'st embarrass him, dear heart,
    Alone, he would not have a fear."

So spake the hermit-monarch blind,
    His wife too, entering in, exprest
The self-same thoughts in words as kind,
    And begged Savitri hard, to rest.
"Thy recent fasts and vigils, child,
    Make thee unfit to undertake
This journey to the forest wild."
    But nothing could her purpose shake.
She urged the nature of her vows,
    Required her now the rites were done
To follow where her loving spouse
    Might e'en a chance of danger run.

"Go then, my child,—we give thee leave,
    But with thy husband quick return,
Before the flickering shades of eve

Deepen to night, and planets burn,
And forest-paths become obscure,
   Lit only by their doubtful rays.
The gods, who guard all women pure,
   Bless thee and kept thee in thy ways,
And safely bring thee and thy lord!"
   On this she left, and swiftly ran
Where with his saw in lieu of sword,
   And basket, plodded Satyavan.

Oh, lovely are the woods at dawn,
   And lovely in the sultry noon,
But loveliest, when the sun withdrawn
   The twilight and a crescent moon
Change all asperities of shape,
   And tone all colours softly down,
With a blue veil of silvered crape!
   Lo! By that hill which palm-trees crown,
Down the deep glade with perfume rife
   From buds that to the dews expand,
The husband and the faithful wife
   Pass to dense jungle,—hand in hand.

Satyavan bears beside his saw
   A forkèd stick to pluck the fruit,
His wife, the basket lined with straw;
   He talks, but she is almost mute,
And very pale. The minutes pass;
   The basket has no further space,
Now on the fruits they flowers amass
   That with their red flush all the place
While twilight lingers; then for wood
   He saws the branches of the trees,
The noise, heard in the solitude,
   Grates on its soft, low harmonies.

And all the while one dreadful thought
   Haunted Savitri's anxious mind,
Which would have fain its stress forgot;

It came as chainless as the wind,
Oft and again: thus on the spot
    Marked with his heart-blood oft comes back
The murdered man, to see the clot!
    Death's final blow,—the fatal wrack
Of every hope, whence will it fall?
    For fall, by Narad's words, it must;
Persistent rising to appall
    This thought its horrid presence thrust.

Sudden the noise is hushed,—a pause!
    Satyavan lets the weapon drop—
Too well Savitri knows the cause,
    He feels not well, the work must stop.
A pain is in his head,—a pain
    As if he felt the cobra's fangs,
He tries to look around,—in vain,
    A mist before his vision hangs;
The trees whirl dizzily around
    In a fantastic fashion wild;
His throat and chest seem iron-bound,
    He staggers, like a sleepy child.

"My head, my head!—Savitri, dear,
    This pain is frightful. Let me lie
Here on the turf." Her voice was clear
    And very calm was her reply,
As if her heart had banished fear:
    "Lean, love, thy head upon my breast,"
And as she helped him, added—"here,
    So shall thou better breathe and rest."
"Ah me, this pain,—'tis getting dark,
    I see no more,—can this be death?
What means this, gods?—Savitri, mark,
    My hands wax cold, and fails my breath."

"It may be but a swoon." "Ah! no—
    Arrows are piercing through my heart,—
Farewell my love! for I must go,

This, this is death." He gave one start
And then lay quiet on her lap,
    Insensible to sight and sound,
Breathing his last. . . The branches flap
    And fireflies glimmer all around;
His head upon her breast; his frame
    Part on her lap, part on the ground,
Thus lies he. Hours pass. Still the same,
    The pair look statues, magic-bound.

Part III

Death in his palace holds his court,
    His messengers move to and fro,
Each of his mission makes report,
    And takes the royal orders,—Lo,
Some slow before his throne appear
    And humbly in the Presence kneel:
"Why hath the Prince not been brought here?
    The hour is past; nor is appeal
Allowed against foregone decree;
    There is the mandate with the seal!
How comes it ye return to me
    Without him? Shame upon your zeal!"

"O King, whom all men fear,—he lies
    Deep in the dark Medhya wood,
We fled from thence in wild surprise,
    And left him in that solitude.
We dared not touch him, for there sits,
    Beside him, lighting all the place,
A woman fair, whose brow permits
    In its austerity of grace
And purity,—no creatures foul
    As we seemed, by her loveliness,
Or soul of evil, ghost or ghoul,
    To venture close, and far, far less

"To stretch a hand, and bear the dead;
    We left her leaning on her hand,
Thoughtful; no tear-drop had she shed,
    But looked the goddess of the land,
With her meek air of mild command."—
    "Then on this errand I must go
Myself, and bear my dreaded brand,
    This duty unto Fate I owe;
I know the merits of the prince,
    But merit saves not from the doom
Common to man; his death long since
    Was destined in his beauty's bloom."

Part IV

As still Savitri sat beside
    Her husband dying,—dying fast,
She saw a stranger slowly glide
    Beneath the boughs that shrunk aghast.
Upon his head he wore a crown
    That shimmered in the doubtful light;
His vestment scarlet reached low down,
    His waist, a golden girdle dight.
His skin was dark as bronze; his face
    Irradiate, and yet severe;
His eyes had much of love and grace,
    But glowed so bright, they filled with fear.

A string was in the stranger's hand
    Noosed at its end. Her terrors now
Savitri scarcely could command.
    Upon the sod beneath a bough,
She gently laid her husband's head,
    And in obeisance bent her brow.
"No mortal form is thine,"—she said,
    "Beseech thee say what god art thou?
And what can be thine errand here?"
    "Savitri, for thy prayers, thy faith,

Thy frequent vows, thy fasts severe,
    I answer,—list,—my name is Death."

"And I am come myself to take
    Thy husband from this earth away,
And he shall cross the doleful lake
    In my own charge, and let me say
To few such honours I accord,
    But his pure life and thine require
No less from me." The dreadful sword
    Like lightning glanced one moment dire;
And then the inner man was tied,
    The soul no bigger than the thumb,
To be borne onwards by his side:—
    Savitri all the while stood dumb.

But when the god moved slowly on
    To gain his own dominions dim,
Leaving the body there—anon
    Savitri meekly followed him,
Hoping against all hope; he turned
    And looked surprised. "Go back, my child!"
Pale, pale the stars above them burned,
    More weird the scene had grown and wild;
"It is not for the living—hear!
    To follow where the dead must go,
Thy duty lies before thee clear,
    What thou shouldst do, the Shasters show."

"The funeral rites that they ordain
    And sacrifices must take up
Thy first sad moments; not in vain
    Is held to thee this bitter cup;
Its lessons thou shall learn in time!
    All that thou *canst* do, thou hast done
For thy dear lord. Thy love sublime
    My deepest sympathy hath won.
Return, for thou hast come as far
    As living creature may. Adieu!

Let duty be thy guiding star,
    As ever. To thyself be true!"

"Where'er my husband dear is led,
    Or journeys of his own free will,
I too must go, though darkness spread
    Across my path, portending ill,
'Tis thus my duty I have read!
    If I am wrong, oh! with me bear;
But do not bid me backward tread
    My way forlorn,—for I can dare
All things but that; ah! pity me,
    A woman frail, too sorely tried!
And let me, let me follow thee,
    O gracious god,—whate'er betide.

"By all things sacred, I entreat,
    By Penitence that purifies,
By prompt Obedience, full, complete,
    To spiritual masters, in the eyes
Of gods so precious, by the love
    I bear my husband, by the faith
That looks from earth to heaven above,
    And by thy own great name O Death,
And all thy kindness, bid me not
    To leave thee, and to go my way,
But let me follow as I ought
    Thy steps and his, as best I may.

"I know that in this transient world
    All is delusion,—nothing true;
I know its shows are mists unfurled
    To please and vanish. To renew
Its bubble joys, be magic bound
    In *Maya's* network frail and fair,
Is not my aim! The gladsome sound
    Of husband, brother, friend, is air
To such as know that all must die,
    And that at last the time must come,

When eye shall speak no more to eye
    And Love cry,—Lo, this is my sum.

"I know in such a world as this
    No one can gain his heart's desire,
Or pass the years in perfect bliss;
    Like gold we must be tried by fire;
And each shall suffer as he acts
    And thinks,—his own sad burden bear;
No friends can help,—his sins are facts
    That nothing can annul or square,
And he must bear their consequence.
    Can I my husband save by rites?
Ah, no,—that were a vain pretence,
    Justice eternal strict requites.

"He for his deeds shall get his due
    As I for mine: thus here each soul
Is its own friend if it pursue
    The right, and run straight for the goal;
But its own worst and direst foe
    If it choose evil, and in tracks
Forbidden, for its pleasure go.
    Who knows not this, true wisdom lacks,
Virtue should be the turn and end
    Of every life, all else is vain,
Duty should be its dearest friend
    If higher life, it would attain."

"So sweet thy words ring on mine ear,
    Gentle Savitri, that I fain
Would give some sign to make it clear
    Thou hast not prayed to me in vain.
Satyavan's life I may not grant,
    Nor take before its term thy life,
But I am not all adamant,
    I feel for thee, thou faithful wife!
Ask thou aught else, and let it be
    Some good thing for thyself or thine,

And I shall give it, child, to thee,
  If any power on earth be mine."

"Well be it so. My husband's sire,
  Hath lost his sight and fair domain,
Give to his eyes their former fire,
  And place him on his throne again."
"It shall be done. Go back, my child,
  The hour wears late, the wind feels cold,
The path becomes more weird and wild,
  Thy feet are torn, there's blood, behold!
Thou feelest faint from weariness,
  Oh try to follow me no more;
Go home, and with thy presence bless
  Those who thine absence there deplore."

"No weariness, O Death, I feel,
  And how should I, when by the side
Of Satyavan? In woe and weal
  To be a helpmate swears the bride.
This is my place; by solemn oath
  Wherever thou conductest him
I too must go, to keep my troth;
  And if the eye at times should brim,
'Tis human weakness, give me strength
  My work appointed to fulfil,
That I may gain the crown at length
  The gods give those who do their will.

"The power of goodness is so great
  We pray to feel its influence
Forever on us. It is late,
  And the strange landscape awes my sense;
But I would fain with thee go on,
  And hear thy voice so true and kind;
The false lights that on objects shone
  Have vanished, and no longer blind,
Thanks to thy simple presence. Now
  I feel a fresher air around,

And see the glory of that brow
   With flashing rubies fitly crowned.

"Men call thee Yama—conqueror,
   Because it is against their will
They follow thee,—and they abhor
   The Truth which thou wouldst aye instil.
If they thy nature knew aright,
   O god, all other gods above!
And that thou conquerest in the fight
   By patience, kindness, mercy, love,
And not by devastating wrath,
   They would not shrink in childlike fright
To see thy shadow on their path,
   But hail thee as sick souls the light."

"Thy words, Savitri, greet mine ear
   As sweet as founts that murmur low
To one who in the deserts drear
   With parchèd tongue moves faint and slow,
Because thy talk is heart-sincere,
   Without hypocrisy or guile;
Demand another boon, my dear,
   But not of those forbad erewhile,
And I shall grant it, ere we part:
   Lo, the stars pale,—the way is long,
Receive thy boon, and homewards start,
   For ah, poor child, thou art not strong."

"Another boon! My sire the king
   Beside myself hath children none,
Oh grant that from his stock may spring
   A hundred boughs." "It shall be done.
He shall be blest with many a son
   Who his old palace shall rejoice."
"Each heart-wish from thy goodness won,
   If I am still allowed a choice,
I fain thy voice would ever hear,
   Reluctant am I still to part,

The way seems short when thou art near
    And Satyavan, my heart's dear heart."

"Of all the pleasures given on earth
    The company of the good is best,
For weariness has never birth
    In such a commerce sweet and blest;
The sun runs on its wonted course,
    The earth its plenteous treasure yields,
All for their sake, and by the force
    Their prayer united ever wields.
Oh let me, let me ever dwell
    Amidst the good, where'er it be,
Whether in lowly hermit-cell
    Or in some spot beyond the sea.

"The favours man accords to men
    Are never fruitless, from them rise
A thousand acts beyond our ken
    That float like incense to the skies;
For benefits can ne'er efface,
    They multiply and widely spread,
And honour follows on their trace.
    Sharp penances, and vigils dread,
Austerities, and wasting fasts,
    Create an empire, and the blest
Long as this spiritual empire lasts
    Become the saviours of the rest."

"O thou endowed with every grace
    And every virtue,—thou whose soul
Appears upon thy lovely face,
    May the great gods who all control
Send thee their peace. I too would give
    One favour more before I go;
Ask something for thyself, and live
    Happy, and dear to all below,
Till summoned to the bliss above.
    Savitri ask, and ask unblamed."—

She took the clue, felt Death was Love,
    For no exceptions now he named,

And boldly said,—"Thou knowest, Lord,
    The inmost hearts and thoughts of all!
There is no need to utter word,
    Upon thy mercy sole, I call.
If speech be needful to obtain
    Thy grace,—oh hear a wife forlorn,
Let my Satyavan live again
    And children unto us be born,
Wise, brave, and valiant." "From thy stock
    A hundred families shall spring
As lasting as the solid rock,
    Each son of thine shall be a king."

As thus he spoke, he loosed the knot
    The soul of Satyavan that bound,
And promised further that their lot
    In pleasant places should be found
Thenceforth, and that they both should live
    Four centuries, to which the name
Of fair Savitri, men would give,—
    And then he vanished in a flame.
"Adieu, great god!" She took the soul,
    No bigger than the human thumb,
And running swift, soon reached her goal,
    Where lay the body stark and dumb.

She lifted it with eager hands
    And as before, when he expired,
She placed the head upon the bands
    That bound her breast which hope new-fired,
And which alternate rose and fell;
    Then placed his soul upon his heart
Whence like a bee it found its cell,
    And lo, he woke with sudden start!
His breath came low at first, then deep,
    With an unquiet look he gazed,

As one awaking from a sleep
    Wholly bewildered and amazed.

Part V

As consciousness came slowly back
    He recognised his loving wife—
"Who was it, Love, through regions black
    Where hardly seemed a sign of life
Carried me bound? Methinks I view
    The dark face yet—a noble face,
He had a robe of scarlet hue,
    And ruby crown; far, far through space
He bore me, on and on, but now,"—
    "Thou hast been sleeping, but the man
With glory on his kingly brow,
    Is gone, thou seest, Satyavan!"

"O my belovèd,—thou art free!
    Sleep which had bound thee fast, hath left
Thine eyelids. Try thyself to be!
    For late of every sense bereft
Thou seemedst in a rigid trance;
    And if thou canst, my love, arise,
Regard the night, the dark expanse
    Spread out before us, and the skies."
Supported by her, looked he long
    Upon the landscape dim outspread,
And like some old remembered song
    The past came back,—a tangled thread.

"I had a pain, as if an asp
    Gnawed in my brain, and there I lay
Silent, for oh! I could but gasp,
    Till someone came that bore away
My spirit into lands unknown:
    Thou, dear, who watchedst beside me,—say
Was it a dream from elfland blown,
    Or very truth,—my doubts to stay."

"O Love, look round,—how strange and dread
     The shadows of the high trees fall,
Homeward our path now let us tread,
     Tomorrow I shall tell thee all."

"Arise! Be strong! Gird up thy loins!
     Think of our parents, dearest friend!
The solemn darkness haste enjoins,
     Not likely is it soon to end.
Hark! Jackals still at distance howl,
     The day, long, long will not appear,
Lo, wild fierce eyes through bushes scowl,
     Summon thy courage, lest I fear.
Was that the tiger's sullen growl?
     What means this rush of many feet?
Can creatures wild so near us prowl?
     Rise up, and hasten homewards, sweet!"

He rose, but could not find the track,
     And then, too well, Savitri knew
His wonted force had not come back.
     She made a fire, and from the dew
Essayed to shelter him. At last
     He nearly was himself again,—
Then vividly rose all the past,
     And with the past, new fear and pain.
"What anguish must my parents feel
     Who wait for me the livelong hours!
Their sore wound let us haste to heal
     Before it festers, past our powers:"

"For broken-hearted, they may die!
     Oh hasten dear,—now I am strong,
No more I suffer, let us fly,
     Ah me! each minute seems so long.
They told me once, they could not live
     Without me, in their feeble age,
Their food and water I must give
     And help them in the last sad stage

Of earthly life, and that Beyond
    In which a son can help by rites.
Oh what a love is theirs—how fond!
    Whom now Despair, perhaps, benights.

"Infirm herself, my mother dear
    Now guides, methinks, the tottering feet
Of my blind father, for they hear
    And hasten eagerly to meet
Our fancied steps. O faithful wife
    Let us on wings fly back again,
Upon their safety hangs my life!"
    He tried his feelings to restrain,
But like some river swelling high
    They swept their barriers weak and vain,
Sudden there burst a fearful cry,
    Then followed tears,—like autumn rain.

Hush! Hark, a sweet voice rises clear!
    A voice of earnestness intense,
"If I have worshipped Thee in fear
    And duly paid with reverence
The solemn sacrifices,—hear!
    Send consolation, and thy peace
Eternal, to our parents dear,
    That their anxieties may cease.
Oh, ever hath I loved Thy truth,
    Therefore on Thee I dare to call,
Help us, this night, and them, for sooth
    Without thy help, we perish all."

She took in hers Satyavan's hand,
    She gently wiped his falling tears,
"This weakness, Love, I understand!
    Courage!" She smiled away his fears.
"Now we shall go, for thou art strong."
    She helped him rise up by her side
And led him like a child along,
    He, wistfully the basket eyed

Laden with fruit and flowers. "Not now,
  Tomorrow we shall fetch it hence."
And so, she hung it on a bough,
  "I'll bear thy saw for our defence."

In one fair hand the saw she took,
  The other with a charming grace
She twined around him, and her look
  She turned upwards to his face.
Thus aiding him she felt anew
  His bosom beat against her own—
More firm his step, more clear his view,
  More self-possessed his words and tone
Became, as swift the minutes past,
  And now the pathway he discerns,
And 'neath the trees, they hurry fast,
  For Hope's fair light before them burns.

Under the faint beams of the stars
  How beautiful appeared the flowers,
Light scarlet, flecked with golden bars
  Of the palâsas,[1] in the bowers
That Nature there herself had made
  Without the aid of man. At times
Trees on their path cast densest shade,
  And nightingales sang mystic rhymes
Their fears and sorrows to assuage.
  Where two paths met, the north they chose,
As leading to the hermitage,
  And soon before them, dim it rose.

Here let us end. For all may guess
  The blind old king received his sight,
And ruled again with gentleness
  The country that was his by right;
And that Savitri's royal sire
  Was blest with many sons,—a race

---

1. *Butea frondosa.*

Whom poets praised for martial fire,
    And every peaceful gift and grace.
As for Savitri, to this day
    Her name is named, when couples wed,
And to the bride the parents say,
    Be thou like her, in heart and head.

II

LAKSHMAN

"Hark! Lakshman! Hark, again that cry!
　　It is,—it is my husband's voice!
Oh hasten, to his succour fly,
　　No more hast thou, dear friend, a choice.
He calls on thee, perhaps his foes
　　Environ him on all sides round,
That wail,—it means death's final throes!
　　Why standest thou, as magic-bound?

"Is this a time for thought,—oh gird
　　Thy bright sword on, and take thy bow!
He heeds not, hears not any word,
　　Evil hangs over us, I know!
Swift in decision, prompt in deed,
　　Brave unto rashness, can this be,
The man to whom all looked at need?
　　Is it my brother, that I see!

"Ah no, and I must run alone,
　　For further here I cannot stay;
Art thou transformed to blind dumb stone!
　　Wherefore this impious, strange delay!
That cry,—that cry,—it seems to ring
　　Still in my ears,—I cannot bear
Suspense; if help we fail to bring
　　His death at least we both can share."

"Oh calm thyself, Videhan Queen,
　　No cause is there for any fear,
Hast thou his prowess never seen?
　　Wipe off for shame that dastard tear!
What being of demonian birth
　　Could ever brave his mighty arm?

Is there a creature on the earth
    That dares to work our hero harm?

"The lion and the grisly bear
    Cower when they see his royal look,
Sun-staring eagles of the air
    His glance of anger cannot brook,
Pythons and cobras at his tread
    To their most secret coverts glide,
Bowed to the dust each serpent head
    Erect before in hooded pride.

"Rakshases, Danavs, demons, ghosts,
    Acknowledge in their hearts his might,
And slink to their remotest coasts,
    In terror at his very sight.
Evil to him! Oh fear it not,
    Whatever foes against him rise!
Banish for aye, the foolish thought,
    And be thyself,—bold, great, and wise.

"He call for help! Canst thou believe
    He like a child would shriek for aid
Or pray for respite or reprieve—
    Not of such metal is he made!
Delusive was that piercing cry,—
    Some trick of magic by the foe;
He has a work,—he cannot die,
    Beseech me not from hence to go.

"For here beside thee, as a guard
    'Twas he commanded me to stay,
And dangers with my life to ward
    If they should come across thy way.
Send me not hence, for in this wood
    Bands scattered of the giants lurk,
Who on their wrongs and vengeance brood,
    And wait the hour their will to work."

"Oh shame! And canst thou make my weal
    A plea for lingering! Now I know
What thou art Lakshman! And I feel
    Far better were an open foe.
Art thou a coward? I have seen
    Thy bearing in the battle-fray
Where flew the death-fraught arrows keen,
    Else had I judged thee so today.

"But then thy leader stood beside!
    Dazzles the cloud when shines the sun,
Reft of his radiance, see it glide
    A shapeless mass of vapours dun;
So of thy courage,—or if not,
    The matter is far darker dyed,
What makes thee loth to leave this spot?
    Is there a motive thou wouldst hide?

"He perishes—well, let him die!
    His wife henceforth shall be mine own!
Can that thought deep imbedded lie
    Within thy heart's most secret zone!
Search well and see! one brother takes
    His kingdom,—one would take his wife!
A fair partition!—But it makes
    Me shudder, and abhor my life.

"Art thou in secret league with those
    Who from his hope the kingdom rent?
A spy from his ignoble foes
    To track him in his banishment?
And wouldst thou at his death rejoice?
    I know thou wouldst, or sure ere now
When first thou heardst that well-known voice
    Thou shouldst have run to aid, I trow.

"Learn this,—whatever comes may come,
    But I shall not survive my Love,—
Of all my thoughts here is the sum!

Witness it gods in heaven above.
If fire can burn, or water drown,
    I follow him:—choose what thou wilt,
Truth with its everlasting crown,
    Or falsehood, treachery, and guilt.

"Remain here, with a vain pretence
    Of shielding me from wrong and shame,
Or go and die in his defence
    And leave behind a noble name.
Choose what thou wilt,—I urge no more,
    My pathway lies before me clear,
I did not know thy mind before,
    I know thee now,—and have no fear."

She said and proudly from him turned,—
    Was this the gentle Sîta? No.
Flames from her eyes shot forth and burned,
    The tears therein had ceased to flow.
"Hear me, O Queen, ere I depart,
    No longer can I bear thy words,
They lacerate my inmost heart
    And torture me, like poisoned swords.

"Have I deserved this at thine hand?
    Of lifelong loyalty and truth
Is this the meed? I understand
    Thy feelings, Sîta, and in sooth
I blame thee not,—but thou mightst be
    Less rash in judgement. Look! I go,
Little I care what comes to me
    Wert thou but safe,—God keep thee so!

"In going hence I disregard
    The plainest orders of my chief,
A deed for me,—a soldier,—hard
    And deeply painful, but thy grief
And language, wild and wrong, allow
    No other course. Mine be the crime,

And mine alone,—but oh, do thou
    Think better of me from this time.

"Here with an arrow, lo, I trace
    A magic circle ere I leave,
No evil thing within this space
    May come to harm thee or to grieve.
Step not, for aught, across the line,
    Whatever thou mayst see or hear,
So shalt thou balk the bad design
    Of every enemy I fear.

"And now farewell! What thou hast said,
    Though it has broken quite my heart,
So that I wish that I were dead—
    I would before, O Queen, we part
Freely forgive, for well I know
    That grief and fear have made thee wild,
We part as friends,—is it not so?"
    And speaking thus,—he sadly smiled.

"And oh ye sylvan gods that dwell
    Among these dim and sombre shades,
Whose voices in the breezes swell
    And blend with noises of cascades,
Watch over Sîta, whom alone
    I leave, and keep her safe from harm,
Till we return unto our own,
    I and my brother, arm in arm.

"For though ill omens round us rise
    And frighten her dear heart, I feel
That he is safe. Beneath the skies
    His equal is not,—and his heel
Shall tread all adversaries down,
    Whoever they may chance to be.—
Farewell, O Sîta! Blessings crown
    And Peace forever rest with thee!"

He said, and straight his weapons took
    His bow and arrows pointed keen,
Kind,—nay, indulgent,—was his look,
    No trace of anger there was seen,
Only a sorrow dark, that seemed
    To deepen his resolve to dare
All dangers. Hoarse the vulture screamed,
    As out he strode with dauntless air.

III

JOGADHYA UMA

"Shell-bracelets ho! Shell-bracelets ho!
    Fair maids and matrons come and buy!"
Along the road, in morning's glow,
    The pedlar raised his wonted cry.
The road ran straight, a red, red line,
    To Khirogram, for cream renowned,
Through pasture-meadows where the kine,
    In knee-deep grass, stood magic bound
And half awake, involved in mist,
    That floated in dun coils profound,
Till by the sudden sunbeams kist
    Rich rainbow hues broke all around.

"Shell-bracelets ho! Shell-bracelets ho!"
    The roadside trees still dripped with dew,
And hung their blossoms like a show.
    Who heard the cry? 'Twas but a few,
A ragged herd-boy, here and there,
    With his long stick and naked feet;
A ploughman wending to his care,
    The field from which he hopes the wheat;
An early traveller, hurrying fast
    To the next town; an urchin slow
Bound for the school; these heard and past,
    Unheeding all,—"Shell-bracelets ho!"

Pellucid spread a lake-like tank
    Beside the road now lonelier still,
High on three sides arose the bank
    Which fruit-trees shadowed at their will;
Upon the fourth side was the Ghat,
    With its broad stairs of marble white,
And at the entrance-arch there sat,

Full face against the morning light,
A fair young woman with large eyes,
    And dark hair falling to her zone,
She heard the pedlar's cry arise,
    And eager seemed his ware to own.

"Shell-bracelets ho! See, maiden see!
    The rich enamel sunbeam-kist!
Happy, oh happy, shalt thou be,
    Let them but clasp that slender wrist;
These bracelets are a mighty charm,
    They keep a lover ever true,
And widowhood avert, and harm,
    Buy them, and thou shalt never rue.
Just try them on!"—She stretched her hand,
    "Oh what a nice and lovely fit!
No fairer hand, in all the land,
    And lo! the bracelet matches it."

Dazzled the pedlar on her gazed
    Till came the shadow of a fear,
While she the bracelet arm upraised
    Against the sun to view more clear.
Oh she was lovely, but her look
    Had something of a high command
That filled with awe. Aside she shook
    Intruding curls by breezes fanned
And blown across her brows and face,
    And asked the price, which when she heard
She nodded, and with quiet grace
    For payment to her home referred.

"And where, O maiden, is thy house?
    But no, that wrist-ring has a tongue,
No maiden art thou, but a spouse,
    Happy, and rich, and fair, and young."
"Far otherwise, my lord is poor,
    And him at home thou shalt not find;
Ask for my father; at the door

Knock loudly; he is deaf, but kind.
Seest thou that lofty gilded spire
    Above these tufts of foliage green?
That is our place; its point of fire
    Will guide thee o'er the tract between."

"That is the temple spire."—"Yes, there
    We live; my father is the priest,
The manse is near, a building fair
    But lowly, to the temple's east.
When thou hast knocked, and seen him, say,
    His daughter, at Dhamaser Ghat,
Shell-bracelets bought from thee today,
    And he must pay so much for that.
Be sure, he will not let thee pass
    Without the value, and a meal,
If he demur, or cry alas!
    No money hath he,—then reveal,"

"Within the small box, marked with streaks
    Of bright vermilion, by the shrine,
The key whereof has lain for weeks
    Untouched, he'll find some coin,—'tis mine.
That will enable him to pay
    The bracelet's price, now fare thee well!"
She spoke, the pedlar went away,
    Charmed with her voice, as by some spell;
While she left lonely there, prepared
    To plunge into the water pure,
And like a rose her beauty bared,
    From all observance quite secure.

Not weak she seemed, nor delicate,
    Strong was each limb of flexile grace,
And full the bust; the mien elate,
    Like hers, the goddess of the chase
On Latmos hill,—and oh, the face
    Framed in its cloud of floating hair,
No painter's hand might hope to trace

The beauty and the glory there!
Well might the pedlar look with awe,
 For though her eyes were soft, a ray
Lit them at times, which kings who saw
 Would never dare to disobey.

Onwards through groves the pedlar sped
 Till full in front the sunlit spire
Arose before him. Paths which led
 To gardens trim in gay attire
Lay all around. And lo! the manse,
 Humble but neat with open door!
He paused, and blest the lucky chance
 That brought his bark to such a shore.
Huge straw ricks, log huts full of grain,
 Sleek cattle, flowers, a tinkling bell,
Spoke in a language sweet and plain,
 "Here smiling Peace and Plenty dwell."

Unconsciously he raised his cry,
 "Shell-bracelets ho!" And at his voice
Looked out the priest, with eager eye,
 And made his heart at once rejoice.
"Ho, *Sankha* pedlar! Pass not by,
 But step thou in, and share the food
Just offered on our altar high,
 If thou art in a hungry mood.
Welcome are all to this repast!
 The rich and poor, the high and low!
Come, wash thy feet, and break thy fast,
 Then on thy journey strengthened go."

"Oh thanks, good priest! Observance due
 And greetings! May thy name be blest!
I came on business, but I knew,
 Here might be had both food and rest
Without a charge; for all the poor
 Ten miles around thy sacred shrine
Know that thou keepest open door,

And praise that generous hand of thine:
But let my errand first be told,
    For bracelets sold to thine this day,
So much thou owest me in gold,
    Hast thou the ready cash to pay?

"The bracelets were enamelled,—so
    The price is high."—"How! Sold to mine?
Who bought them, I should like to know."
    "Thy daughter, with the large black eyne,
Now bathing at the marble ghat."
    Loud laughed the priest at this reply,
"I shall not put up, friend, with that;
    No daughter in the world have I,
An only son is all my stay;
    Some minx has played a trick, no doubt,
But cheer up, let thy heart be gay.
    Be sure that I shall find her out."

"Nay, nay, good father, such a face
    Could not deceive, I must aver;
At all events, she knows thy place,
    'And if my father should demur
To pay thee'—thus she said,—'or cry
    He has no money, tell him straight
The box vermilion-streaked to try,
    That's near the shrine.'" "Well, wait, friend, wait!"
The priest said thoughtful, and he ran
    And with the open box came back,
"Here is the price exact, my man,
    No surplus over, and no lack."

"How strange! How strange! Oh blest art thou
    To have beheld her, touched her hand,
Before whom Vishnu's self must bow,
    And Brahma and his heavenly band!
Here have I worshipped her for years
    And never seen the vision bright;
Vigils and fasts and secret tears

Have almost quenched my outward sight;
And yet that dazzling form and face
    I have not seen, and thou, dear friend,
To thee, unsought for, comes the grace,
    What may its purport be, and end?

"How strange! How strange! Oh happy thou!
    And couldst thou ask no other boon
Than thy poor bracelet's price? That brow
    Resplendent as the autumn moon
Must have bewildered thee, I trow,
    And made thee lose thy senses all."
A dim light on the pedlar now
    Began to dawn; and he let fall
His bracelet basket in his haste,
    And backward ran the way he came;
What meant the vision fair and chaste,
    Whose eyes were they,—those eyes of flame?

Swift ran the pedlar as a hind,
    The old priest followed on his trace,
They reached the Ghat but could not find
    The lady of the noble face.
The birds were silent in the wood,
    The lotus flowers exhaled a smell
Faint, over all the solitude,
    A heron as a sentinel
Stood by the bank. They called,—in vain,
    No answer came from hill or fell,
The landscape lay in slumber's chain,
    E'en Echo slept within her cell.

Broad sunshine, yet a hush profound!
    They turned with saddened hearts to go;
Then from afar there came a sound
    Of silver bells;—the priest said low,
"O Mother, Mother, deign to hear,
    The worship-hour has rung; we wait
In meek humility and fear.

Must we return home desolate?
Oh come, as late thou cam'st unsought,
  Or was it but an idle dream?
Give us some sign if it was not,
  A word, a breath, or passing gleam."

Sudden from out the water sprung
  A rounded arm, on which they saw
As high the lotus buds among
  It rose, the bracelet white, with awe.
Then a wide ripple tost and swung
  The blossoms on that liquid plain,
And lo! the arm so fair and young
  Sank in the waters down again.
They bowed before the mystic Power,
  And as they home returned in thought,
Each took from thence a lotus flower
  In memory of the day and spot.

Years, centuries, have passed away,
  And still before the temple shrine
Descendants of the pedlar pay
  Shell bracelets of the old design
As annual tribute. Much they own
  In lands and gold,—but they confess
From that eventful day alone
  Dawned on their industry,—success.
Absurd may be the tale I tell,
  Ill-suited to the marching times,
I loved the lips from which it fell,
  So let it stand among my rhymes.

IV

The Royal Ascetic and the Hind

From the Vishnu Purana. B. II. Chap. XIII

MAITREYA: Of old thou gav'st a promise to relate
The deeds of Bharat, that great hermit-king:
Beloved Master, now the occasion suits,
And I am all attention.
    PARASARA: Brahman, hear.
With a mind fixed intently on his gods
Long reigned in Saligram of ancient fame,
The mighty monarch of the wide, wide world.
Chief of the virtuous, never in his life
Harmed he, or strove to harm, his fellow-man,
Or any creature sentient. But he left
His kingdom in the forest-shades to dwell,
And changed his sceptre for a hermit's staff,
And with ascetic rites, privations rude,
And constant prayers, endeavoured to attain
Perfect dominion on his soul. At morn,
Fuel, and flowers, and fruit, and holy grass,
He gathered for oblations; and he passed
In stern devotions all his other hours;
Of the world heedless, and its myriad cares,
And heedless too of wealth, and love, and fame.

Once on a time, while living thus, he went
To bathe where through the wood the river flows:
And his ablutions done, he sat him down
Upon the shelving bank to muse and pray.
Thither impelled by thirst a graceful hind,
Big with its young, came fearlessly to drink.
Sudden, while yet she drank, the lion's roar,
Feared by all creatures, like a thunder-clap
Burst in that solitude from a thicket nigh.

Startled, the hind leapt up, and from her womb
Her offspring tumbled in the rushing stream.
Whelmed by the hissing waves and carried far
By the strong current swoln by recent rain,
The tiny thing still struggled for its life,
While its poor mother, in her fright and pain,
Fell down upon the bank, and breathed her last.
Up rose the hermit-monarch at the sight
Full of keen anguish; with his pilgrim staff
He drew the new-born creature from the wave;
'Twas panting fast, but life was in it still.
Now, as he saw its luckless mother dead,
He would not leave it in the woods alone,
But with the tenderest pity brought it home.

There, in his leafy hut, he gave it food,
And daily nourished it with patient care,
Until it grew in stature and in strength,
And to the forest skirts could venture forth
In search of sustenance. At early morn
Thenceforth it used to leave the hermitage
And with the shades of evening come again,
And in the little courtyard of the hut
Lie down in peace, unless the tigers fierce,
Prowling about, compelled it to return
Earlier at noon. But whether near or far,
Wandering abroad, or resting in its home,
The monarch-hermit's heart was with it still,
Bound by affection's ties; nor could he think
Of anything besides this little hind,
His nursling. Though a kingdom he had left,
And children, and a host of loving friends,
Almost without a tear, the fount of love
Sprang out anew within his blighted heart,
To greet this dumb, weak, helpless foster-child,
And so, whene'er it lingered in the wilds,
Or at the customed hour could not return,
His thoughts went with it; "And alas!" he cried,
"Who knows, perhaps some lion or some wolf,

Or ravenous tiger with relentless jaws
Already hath devoured it,—timid thing!
Lo, how the earth is dinted with its hoofs,
And variegated. Surely for my joy
It was created. When will it come back,
And rub its budding antlers on my arms
In token of its love and deep delight
To see my face? The shaven stalks of grass,
Kusha and kasha, by its new teeth clipped,
Remind me of it, as they stand in lines
Like pious boys who chant the Samga Veds
Shorn by their vows of all their wealth of hair."
Thus passed the monarch-hermit's time; in joy,
With smiles upon his lips, whenever near
His little favourite; in bitter grief
And fear, and trouble, when it wandered far.
And he who had abandoned ease and wealth,
And friends and dearest ties, and kingly power,
Found his devotions broken by the love
He had bestowed upon a little hind
Thrown in his way by chance. Years glided on. . .
And Death, who spareth none, approached at last
The hermit-king to summon him away;
The hind was at his side, with tearful eyes
Watching his last sad moments, like a child
Beside a father. He too, watched and watched
His favourite through a blinding film of tears,
And could not think of the Beyond at hand,
So keen he felt the parting, such deep grief
O'erwhelmed him for the creature he had reared.
To it devoted was his last, last thought,
Reckless of present and of future both!

Thus far the pious chronicle, writ of old
By Brahman sage; but we, who happier, live
Under the holiest dispensation, know
That God is Love, and not to be adored
By a devotion born of stoic pride,
Or with ascetic rites, or penance hard,

But with a love, in character akin
To His unselfish, all-including love.
And therefore little can we sympathize
With what the Brahman sage would fain imply
As the concluding moral of his tale,
That for the hermit-king it was a sin
To love his nursling. What! a sin to love!
A sin to pity! Rather should we deem
Whatever Brahmans wise, or monks may hold,
That he had sinned in *casting off* all love
By his retirement to the forest-shades;
For that was to abandon duties high,
And, like a recreant soldier, leave the post
Where God had placed him as a sentinel.

This little hind brought strangely on his path,
This love engendered in his withered heart,
This hindrance to his rituals,—might these not
Have been ordained to teach him? Call him back
To ways marked out for him by Love divine?
And with a mindless self-willed to adore?

Not in seclusion, not apart from all,
Not in a place elected for its peace,
But in the heat and bustle of the world,
'Mid sorrow, sickness, suffering and sin,
Must he still labour with a loving soul
Who strives to enter through the narrow gate.

V

The Legend of Dhruva

Vishnu Purana. Book I. Chapter XI

Sprung from great Brahma, Manu had two sons,
Heroic and devout, as I have said,
Pryavrata and Uttanapado,—names
Known in legends; and of these the last
Married two wives, Suruchee, his adored,
The mother of a handsome petted boy
Uttama; and Suneetee, less beloved,
The mother of another son whose name
Was Dhruva. Seated on his throne the king
Uttanapado, on his knee one day
Had placed Uttama; Dhruva, who beheld
His brother in that place of honour, longed
To clamber up and by his playmate sit;
Led on by Love he came, but found, alas!
Scant welcome and encouragement; the king
Saw fair Suruchee sweep into the hall
With stately step,—aye, every inch a queen,
And dared not smile upon her co-wife's son.
Observing him,—her rival's boy,—intent
To mount ambitious to his father's knee,
Where sat her own, thus fair Suruchee spake:
"Why hast thou, child, formed such a vain design?
Why harboured such an aspiration proud,
Born from another's womb and not from mine?
Oh thoughtless! To desire the loftiest place,
The throne of thrones, a royal father's lap!
It is an honour to the destined given,
And not within thy reach. What though thou art
Born of the king; those sleek and tender limbs
Hold of my blood no portion; I am queen.
To be the equal of mine only son

Were in thee vain ambition. Know'st thou not,
Fair prattler, thou art sprung,—not, not from mine,
But from Suneetee's bowels? Learn thy place."

Repulsed in silence from his father's lap,
Indignant, furious, at the words that fell
From his step-mother's lips, poor Dhruva ran
To his own mother's chambers, where he stood
Beside her with his pale, thin, trembling lips,
(Trembling with an emotion ill-suppressed)
And hair in wild disorder, till she took
And raised him to her lap, and gently said:
"Oh, child, what means this? What can be the cause
Of this great anger? Who hath given thee pain?
He that hath vexed thee, hath despised thy sire,
For in these veins thou hast the royal blood."

Thus conjured, Dhruva, with a swelling heart
Repeated to his mother every word
That proud Suruchee spake, from first to last,
Even in the very presence of the king.

His speech oft broken by his tears and sobs,
Helpless Suneetee, languid-eyed from care,
Heard sighing deeply, and then soft replied:
"Oh son, to lowly fortune thou wert born,
And what my co-wife said to thee is truth;
No enemy to Heaven's favoured ones may say
Such words as thy step-mother said to thee.
Yet, son, it is not meet that thou shouldst grieve
Or vex thy soul. The deeds that thou hast done,
The evil, haply, in some former life,
Long, long ago, who may alas! annul,
Or who the good works not done, supplement!
The sins of previous lives must bear their fruit.
The ivory throne, the umbrella of gold,
The best steed, and the royal elephant
Rich caparisoned, must be his by right
Who has deserved them by his virtuous acts

In times long past. Oh think on this, my son,
And be content. For glorious actions done
Not in this life, but in some previous birth,
Suruchee by the monarch is beloved.
Women, unfortunate like myself, who bear
Only the name of wife without the powers,
But pine and suffer for our ancient sins.
Suruchee raised her virtues pile on pile,
Hence Uttama her son, the fortunate!
Suneetee heaped but evil,—hence her son
Dhruva the luckless! But for all this, child,
It is not meet that thou shouldst ever grieve
As I have said. That man is truly wise
Who is content with what he has, and seeks
Nothing beyond, but in whatever sphere,
Lowly or great, God placed him, works in faith;
My son, my son, though proud Suruchee spake
Harsh words indeed, and hurt thee to the quick,
Yet to thine eyes thy duty should be plain.
Collect a large sum of the virtues; thence
A goodly harvest must to thee arise.
Be meek, devout, and friendly, full of love,
Intent to do good to the human race
And to all creatures sentient made of God;
And oh, be humble, for on modest worth
Descends prosperity, even as water flows
Down to low grounds."

                    She finished, and her son,
Who patiently had listened, thus replied:—

"Mother, thy words of consolation find
 Nor resting-place, nor echo in this heart
 Broken by words severe, repulsing Love
 That timidly approached to worship. Hear
 My resolve unchangeable. I shall try
 The highest good, the loftiest place to win,
 Which the whole world deems priceless and desires.
 There is a crown above my father's crown,

I shall obtain it, and at any cost
Of toil, or penance, or unceasing prayer.
Not born of proud Suruchee, whom the king
Favours and loves, but grown up from a germ
In thee, O mother, humble as thou art,
I yet shall show thee what is in my power.
Thou shalt behold my glory and rejoice.
Let Uttama my brother,—not thy son,—
Receive the throne and royal titles,—all
My father pleases to confer on him.
I grudge them not. Not with another's gifts
Desire I, dearest mother, to be rich,
But with my own work would acquire a name.
And I shall strive unceasing for a place
Such as my father hath not won,—a place
That would not know him even,—aye, a place
Far, far above the highest of this earth."

He said, and from his mother's chambers past,
And went into the wood where hermits live,
And never to his father's house returned.

Well kept the boy his promise made that day!
By prayer and penance Dhruva gained at last
The highest heavens, and there he shines a star!
Nightly men see him in the firmament.

TORU DUTT

VI

BUTTOO

"Ho! Master of the wondrous art!
 Instruct me in fair archery,
 And buy for aye,—a grateful heart
 That will not grudge to give thy fee."
 Thus spoke a lad with kindling eyes,
 A hunter's low-born son was he,—
 To Dronacharjya, great and wise,
 Who sat with princes round his knee.

 Up Time's fair stream far back,—oh far,
 The great wise teacher must be sought!
 The Kurus had not yet in war
 With the Pandava brethren fought.
 In peace, at Dronacharjya's feet,
 Magic and archery they learned,
 A complex science, which we meet
 No more, with ages past inurned.

"And who art thou," the teacher said,
"My science brave to learn so fain?
 Which many kings who wear the thread
 Have asked to learn of me in vain."
"My name is Buttoo," said the youth,
"A hunter's son, I know not Fear";
 The teacher answered, smiling smooth,
"Then know him from this time, my dear."

 Unseen the magic arrow came,
 Amidst the laughter and the scorn
 Of royal youths,—like lightning flame
 Sudden and sharp. They blew the horn,
 As down upon the ground he fell,
 Not hurt, but made a jest and game;—

He rose,—and waved a proud farewell,
But cheek and brow grew red with shame.

And lo,—a single, single tear
  Dropped from his eyelash as he past,
"My place I gather is not here;
  No matter,—what is rank or caste?
In us is honour, or disgrace,
  Not out of us," 'twas thus he mused,
"The question is,—not wealth or place,
  But gifts well used, or gifts abused."

"And I shall do my best to gain
  The science that man will not teach,
For life is as a shadow vain,
  Until the utmost goal we reach
To which the soul points. I shall try
  To realize my waking dream,
And what if I should chance to die?
  None miss one bubble from a stream."

So thinking, on and on he went,
  Till he attained the forest's verge,
The garish day was well-nigh spent,
  Birds had already raised its dirge.
Oh what a scene! How sweet and calm!
  It soothed at once his wounded pride,
And on his spirit shed a balm
  That all its yearnings purified.

What glorious trees! The sombre saul
  On which the eye delights to rest,
The betel-nut,—a pillar tall,
  With feathery branches for a crest,
The light-leaved tamarind spreading wide,
  The pale faint-scented bitter neem,
The seemul, gorgeous as a bride,
  With flowers that have the ruby's gleam,

The Indian fig's pavilion tent
In which whole armies might repose,
With here and there a little rent,
The sunset's beauty to disclose,
The bamboo boughs that sway and swing
'Neath bulbuls as the south wind blows,
The mangoe-tope, a close dark ring,
Home of the rooks and clamorous crows,

The champac, bok, and South-sea pine,
The nagessur with pendant flowers
Like ear-rings,—and the forest vine
That clinging over all, embowers,
The sirish famed in Sanscrit song
Which rural maidens love to wear,
The peepul giant-like and strong,
The bramble with its matted hair,

All these, and thousands, thousands more,
With helmet red, or golden crown,
Or green tiara, rose before
The youth in evening's shadows brown.
He passed into the forest,—there
New sights of wonder met his view,
A waving Pampas green and fair
All glistening with the evening dew.

How vivid was the breast-high grass!
Here waved in patches, forest corn,—
Here intervened a deep morass,—
Here arid spots of verdure shorn
Lay open,—rock or barren sand,—
And here again the trees arose
Thick clustering,—a glorious band
Their tops still bright with sunset glows.—

Stirred in the breeze the crowding boughs,
And seemed to welcome him with signs,

Onwards and on,—till Buttoo's brows
Are gemmed with pearls, and day declines.
Then in a grassy open space
He sits and leans against a tree,
To let the wind blow on his face
And look around him leisurely.

Herds, and still herds, of timid deer
Were feeding in the solitude,
They knew not man, and felt no fear,
And heeded not his neighbourhood,
Some young ones with large eyes and sweet
Came close, and rubbed their foreheads smooth
Against his arms, and licked his feet,
As if they wished his cares to soothe.

"They touch me," he exclaimed with joy,
"They have no pride of caste like men,
They shrink not from the hunter-boy,
Should not my home be with them then?
Here in this forest let me dwell,
With these companions innocent,
And learn each science and each spell
All by myself in banishment."

"A calm, calm life,—and it shall be
Its own exceeding great reward!
No thoughts to vex in all I see,
No jeers to bear or disregard;—
All creatures and inanimate things
Shall be my tutors; I shall learn
From beast, and fish, and bird with wings,
And rock, and stream, and tree, and fern."

With this resolve, he soon began
To build a hut, of reeds and leaves,
And when that needful work was done
He gathered in his store, the sheaves
Of forest corn, and all the fruit,

Date, plum, guava, he could find,
And every pleasant nut and root
By Providence for man designed,

A statue next of earth he made,
An image of the teacher wise,
So deft he laid, the light and shade,
On figure, forehead, face and eyes,
That anyone who chanced to view
That image tall might soothly swear,
If he great Dronacharjya knew,
The teacher in his flesh was there.

Then at the statue's feet he placed
A bow, and arrows tipped with steel,
With wild-flower garlands interlaced,
And hailed the figure in his zeal
As Master, and his head he bowed,
A pupil reverent from that hour
Of one who late had disallowed
The claim, in pride of place and power.

By strainèd sense, by constant prayer,
By steadfastness of heart and will,
By courage to confront and dare,
All obstacles he conquered still;
A conscience clear,—a ready hand,
Joined to a meek humility,
Success must everywhere command,
How could he fail who had all three!

And now, by tests assured, he knows
His own God-gifted wondrous might,
Nothing to any man he owes,
Unaided he has won the fight;
Equal to gods themselves,—above
Wishmo and Drona,—for his worth
His name, he feels, shall be with love
Reckoned with great names of the earth.

Yet lacks he not, in reverence
To Dronacharjya, who declined
To teach him,—nay, with e'en offence
That well might wound a noble mind,
Drove him away;—for in his heart
Meek, placable, and ever kind,
Resentment had not any part,
And Malice never was enshrined.

One evening, on his work intent,
Alone he practised Archery,
When lo! the bow proved false and sent
The arrow from its mark awry;
Again he tried,—and failed again;
Why was it? Hark!—A wild dog's bark!
An evil omen:—it was plain
Some evil on his path hung dark!

Thus many times he tried and failed,
And still that lean, persistent dog
At distance, like some spirit wailed,
Safe in the cover of a fog.
His nerves unstrung, with many a shout
He strove to frighten it away,
It would not go,—but roamed about,
Howling, as wolves howl for their prey.

Worried and almost in a rage,
One magic shaft at last he sent,
A sample of his science sage,
To quiet but the noises meant.
Unerring to its goal it flew,
No death ensued, no blood was dropped,
But by the hush the young man knew
At last that howling noise had stopped.

It happened on this very day
That the Pandava princes came
With all the Kuru princes gay

To beat the woods and hunt the game.
Parted from others in the chase,
Arjuna brave the wild dog found,—
Stuck still the shaft,—but not a trace
Of hurt, though tongue and lip were bound.

"Wonder of wonders! Didst not thou
O Dronacharjya, promise me
Thy crown in time should deck my brow
And I be first in archery?
Lo! here, someother thou hast taught
A magic spell,—to all unknown;
Who has in secret from thee bought
The knowledge, in this arrow shown!"

Indignant thus Arjuna spake
To his great Master when they met—
"My word, my honour, is at stake,
Judge not, Arjuna, judge not yet.
Come, let us see the dog,"—and straight
They followed up the creature's trace.
They found it, in the selfsame state,
Dumb, yet unhurt,—near Buttoo's place.

A hut,—a statue,—and a youth
In the dim forest,—what mean these?
They gazed in wonder, for in sooth
The thing seemed full of mysteries.
"Now who art thou that dar'st to raise
Mine image in the wilderness?
Is it for worship and for praise?
What is thine object? speak, confess."

"Oh Master, unto thee I came
To learn thy science. Name or pelf
I had not, so was driven with shame,
And here I learn all by myself.
But still as Master thee revere,
For who so great in archery!

Lo, all my inspiration here,
And all my knowledge is from thee."

"If I am Master, now thou hast
   Finished thy course, give me my due.
   Let all the past, be dead and past,
   Henceforth be ties between us new."
"All that I have, O Master mine,
   All I shall conquer by my skill,
   Gladly shall I to thee resign,
   Let me but know thy gracious will."

"Is it a promise?" "Yea, I swear
   So long as I have breath and life
   To give thee all thou wilt." "Beware!
   Rash promise ever ends in strife."
"Thou art my Master,—ask! oh ask!
   From thee my inspiration came,
   Thou canst not set too hard a task,
   Nor aught refuse I, free from blame."

"If it be so,—Arjuna hear!"
   Arjuna and the youth were dumb,
"For thy sake, loud I ask and clear,
   Give me, O youth, thy right-hand thumb.
   I promised in my faithfulness
   No equal ever shall there be
   To thee, Arjuna,—and I press
   For this sad recompense—for thee."

Glanced the sharp knife one moment high,
   The severed thumb was on the sod,
   There was no tear in Buttoo's eye,
   He left the matter with his God.
"For this,"—said Dronacharjya,—"Fame
   Shall sound thy praise from sea to sea,
   And men shall ever link thy name
   With Self-help, Truth, and Modesty."

VII

SINDHU

Part I

Deep in the forest shades there dwelt
    A *Muni* and his wife,
Blind, gray-haired, weak, they hourly felt
    Their slender hold on life.

No friends had they, no help or stay,
    Except an only boy,
A bright-eyed child, his laughter gay,
    Their leaf-hut filled with joy.

Attentive, duteous, loving, kind,
    Thoughtful, sedate, and calm,
He waited on his parents blind,
    Whose days were like a psalm.

He roamed the woods for luscious fruits,
    He brought them water pure,
He cooked their simple mess of roots,
    Content to live obscure.

To fretful questions, answers mild
    He meekly ever gave,
If they reproved, he only smiled,
    He loved to be their slave.

Not that to him they were austere,
    But age is peevish still,
Dear to their hearts he was,—so dear,
    That none his place might fill.

They called him Sindhu, and his name
    Was ever on their tongue,
And he, nor cared for wealth nor fame,
    Who dwelt his own among.

A belt of *Bela* trees hemmed round
    The cottage small and rude,
If peace on earth was ever found
    'Twas in that solitude.

Part II

Great Dasarath, the King of Oude,
    Whom all men love and fear,
With elephants and horses proud
    Went forth to hunt the deer.

Oh gallant was the long array!
    Pennons and plumes were seen,
And swords that mirrored back the day,
    And spears and axes keen.

Rang trump, and conch, and piercing fife,
    Woke Echo from her bed!
The solemn woods with sounds were rife
    As on the pageant sped.

Hundreds, nay thousands, on they went!
    The wild beasts fled away!
Deer ran in herds, and wild boars spent
    Became an easy prey.

Whirring the peacocks from the brake
    With Argus wings arose,
Wild swans abandoned pool and lake
    For climes beyond the snows.

From tree to tree the monkeys sprung,
    Unharmed and unpursued,

As louder still the trumpets rung
    And startled all the wood.

The porcupines and such small game
    Unnoted fled at will,
The weasel only caught to tame
    From fissures in the hill.

Slunk light the tiger from the bank,
    But sudden turned to bay!
When he beheld the serried rank
    That barred his tangled way.

Uprooting fig-trees on their path,
    And trampling shrubs and flowers,
Wild elephants, in fear and wrath,
    Burst through, like moving towers.

Lowering their horns in crescents grim
    Whene'er they turned about,
Retreated into coverts dim
    The bisons' fiercer rout.

And in this mimic game of war
    In bands dispersed and past
The royal train,—some near, some far,
    As day closed in at last.

Where was the king? He left his friends
    At midday, it was known,
And now that evening fast descends
    Where was he? All alone.

Curving, the river formed a lake,
    Upon whose bank he stood,
No noise the silence there to break,
    Or mar the solitude.

Upon the glassy surface fell
    The last beams of the day,
Like fiery darts, that lengthening swell,
    As breezes wake and play.

Osiers and willows on the edge
    And purple buds and red,
Leant down,—and 'mid the pale green sedge
    The lotus raised its head.

And softly, softly, hour by hour
    Light faded, and a veil
Fell over tree, and wave, and flower,
    On came the twilight pale.

Deeper and deeper grew the shades,
    Stars glimmered in the sky,
The nightingale along the glades
    Raised her preluding cry.

What is that momentary flash?
    A gleam of silver scales
Reveals the *Mahseer*;—then a splash,
    And calm again prevails.

As darkness settled like a pall
    The eye would pierce in vain,
The fireflies gemmed the bushes all,
    Like fiery drops of rain.

Pleased with the scene,—and knowing not
    Which way, alas! to go,
The monarch lingered on the spot,—
    The lake spread bright below.

He lingered, when—oh hark! oh hark
    What sound salutes his ear!
A roebuck drinking in the dark,
    Not hunted, nor in fear.

Straight to the stretch his bow he drew,
    That bow ne'er missed its aim,
Whizzing the deadly arrow flew,
    Ear-guided, on the game!

Ah me! What means this?—Hark, a cry,
    A feeble human wail,
"Oh God!" it said—"I die,—I die,
    Who'll carry home the pail?"

Startled, the monarch forward ran,
    And then there met his view
A sight to freeze in any man
    The warm blood coursing true.

A child lay dying on the grass,
    A pitcher by his side,
Poor Sindhu was the child, alas!
    His parents' stay and pride.

His bow and quiver down to fling,
    And lift the wounded boy,
A moment's work was with the king.
    Not dead,—that was a joy!

He placed the child's head on his lap,
    And ranged the blinding hair,
The blood welled fearful from the gap
    On neck and bosom fair.

He dashed cold water on the face,
    He chafed the hands, with sighs,
Till sense revived, and he could trace
    Expression in the eyes.

Then mingled with his pity, fear—
    In all this universe
What is so dreadful as to hear
    A Bramin's dying curse!

So thought the king, and on his brow
  The beads of anguish spread,
And Sindhu, fully conscious now,
  The anguish plainly read.

"What dost thou fear, O mighty king?
  For sure a king thou art!
Why should thy bosom anguish wring?
  No crime was in thine heart!

"Unwittingly the deed was done;
  It is my destiny,
O fear not thou, but pity one
  Whose fate is thus to die.

"No curses, no!—I bear no grudge,
  Not thou my blood hast spilt,
Lo! here before the unseen Judge,
  Thee I absolve from guilt.

"The iron, red-hot as it burns,
  Burns those that touch it too,
Not such my nature,—for it spurns,
  Thank God, the like to do.

"Because I suffer, should I give
  Thee, king, a needless pain?
Ah, no! I die, but mayst thou live,
  And cleansed from every stain!"

Struck with these words, and doubly grieved
  At what his hands had done,
The monarch wept, as weeps bereaved
  A man his only son.

"Nay, weep not so," resumed the child,
  "But rather let me say
My own sad story, sin-defiled.
  And why I die today!"

"Picking a living in our sheaves,
      And happy in their loves,
Near, 'mid a peepul's quivering leaves,
      There lived a pair of doves.

"Never were they two separate,
      And lo, in idle mood,
I took a sling and ball, elate
      In wicked sport and rude,—

"And killed one bird,—it was the male,
      Oh cruel deed and base!
The female gave a plaintive wail
      And looked me in the face!

"The wail and sad reproachful look
      In plain words seemed to say,
A widowed life I cannot brook,
      The forfeit thou must pay.

"What was my darling's crime that thou
      Him wantonly shouldst kill?
The curse of blood is on thee now,
      Blood calls for red blood still.

"And so I die—a bloody death—
      But not for this I mourn,
To feel the world pass with my breath
      I gladly could have borne,

"But for my parents, who are blind,
      And have no other stay,—
This, this, weighs sore upon my mind
      And fills me with dismay.

"Upon the eleventh day of the moon
      They keep a rigorous fast,
All yesterday they fasted; soon
      For water and repast.

"They shall upon me feebly call!
    Ah, must they call in vain?
Bear thou the pitcher, friend—'tis all
    I ask—down that steep lane."

He pointed,—ceased,—then sudden died!
    The king took up the corpse,
And with the pitcher slowly hied,
    Attended by Remorse.

Down the steep lane—unto the hut
    Girt round with *Bela* trees;
Gleamed far a light-the door not shut
    Was open to the breeze.

Part III

"Oh why does not our child return?
    Too long he surely stays."—
Thus to the *Muni*, blind and stern,
    His partner gently says.

"For fruits and water when he goes
    He never stays so long,
Oh can it be, beset by foes,
    He suffers cruel wrong?

"Some distance he has gone, I fear,
    A more circuitous round,—
Yet why should he? The fruits are near,
    The river near our bound.

"I die of thirst,—it matters not
    If Sindhu be but safe,
What if he leave us, and this spot,
    Poor birds in cages chafe.

"Peevish and fretful oft we are,—
    Ah, no—that cannot be:

Of our blind eyes he is the star,
    Without him, what were we?

"Too much he loves us to forsake,
    But something ominous,
Here in my heart, a dreadful ache,
    Says, he is gone from us.

"Why do my bowels for him yearn,
    What ill has crossed his path?
Blind, helpless, whither shall we turn,
    Or how avert the wrath?

"Lord of my soul—what means my pain?
    This horrid terror,—like
Some cloud that hides a hurricane;
    Hang not, O lightning,—strike!"

Thus while she spake, the king drew near
    With haggard look and wild,
Weighed down with grief, and pale with fear,
    Bearing the lifeless child.

Rustled the dry leaves neath his foot,
    And made an eerie sound,
A neighbouring owl began to hoot,
    All else was still around.

At the first rustle of the leaves
    The *Muni* answered clear,
"Lo, here he is—oh wherefore grieves
    Thy soul, my partner dear?"

The words distinct, the monarch heard,
    He could no further go,
His nature to its depths was stirred,
    He stopped in speechless woe.

No steps advanced,—the sudden pause
    Attention quickly drew,
Rolled sightless orbs to learn the cause,
    But, hark!—the steps renew.

"Where art thou, darling—why so long
    Hast thou delayed tonight?
We die of thirst,—we are not strong,
    This fasting kills outright.

"Speak to us, dear one,—only speak,
    And calm our idle fears,
Where hast thou been, and what to seek?
    Have pity on these tears."

With head bent low the monarch heard,
    Then came a cruel throb
That tore his heart,—still not a word,
    Only a stifled sob!

"It is not Sindhu—who art thou?
    And where is Sindhu gone?
There's blood upon thy hands—avow!"
    "There is."—"Speak on, speak on."

The dead child in their arms he placed,
    And briefly told his tale,
The parents their dead child embraced,
    And kissed his forehead pale.

"Our hearts are broken. Come, dear wife,
    On earth no more we dwell;
Now welcome Death, and farewell Life,
    And thou, O king, farewell!

"We do not curse thee, God forbid
    But to my inner eye
The future is no longer hid,
    Thou too shalt like us die.

"Die—for a son's untimely loss!
    Die—with a broken heart!
Now help us to our bed of moss,
    And let us both depart."

Upon the moss he laid them down,
    And watched beside the bed;
Death gently came and placed a crown
    Upon each reverend head.

Where the Sarayu's waves dash free
    Against a rocky bank,
The monarch had the corpses three
    Conveyed by men of rank;

There honoured he with royal pomp
    Their funeral obsequies,—
Incense and sandal, drum and tromp,
    And solemn sacrifice.

What is the sequel of the tale?
    How died the king?—Oh man,
A prophet's words can never fail—
    Go, read the Ramayan.

VIII

PREHLAD

A terror both of gods and men
Was Heerun Kasyapu, the king;
No bear more sullen in its den,
No tiger quicker at the spring.
In strength of limb he had not met,
Since first his black flag he unfurled,
Nor in audacious courage, yet,
His equal in the wide, wide world.

The holy Veds he tore in shreds;
Libations, sacrifices, rites,
He made all penal; and the heads
Of Bramins slain, he flung to kites,
"I hold the sceptre in my hand,
I sit upon the ivory throne,
Bow down to me—'tis my command,
And worship me, and me alone."

"No god has ever me withstood,
Why raise ye altars?—cease your pains!
I shall protect you, give you food,
If ye obey,—or else the chains."
Fled at such edicts, self-exiled,
The Bramins and the pundits wise,
To live thenceforth in forests wild,
Or caves in hills that touch the skies.

In secret there, they altars raised,
And made oblations due by fire,
Their gods, their wonted gods, they praised,
Lest these should earth destroy in ire;
They read the Veds, they prayed and mused,
Full well they knew that Time would bring

For favours scorned, and gifts misused,
Undreamt of changes on his wing.

Time changes deserts bare to meads,
And fertile meads to deserts bare,
Cities to pools, and pools with reeds
To towns and cities large and fair.
Time changes purple into rags,
And rags to purple. Chime by chime,
Whether it flies, or runs, or drags—
The wise wait patiently on Time.

Time brought the tyrant children four,
Rahd, Onoorahd, Prehlad, Sunghrad,
Who made his castle gray and hoar,
Once full of gloom, with sunshine glad.
No boys were e'er more beautiful,
No brothers e'er loved more each other,
No sons were e'er more dutiful,
Nor ever kissed a fonder mother.

Nor less beloved were they of him
Who gave them birth, Kasyapu proud,
But made by nature stern and grim,
His love was covered by a cloud
From which it rarely e'er emerged,
To gladden these sweet human flowers.
They grew apace, and now Time urged
The education of their powers.

Who should their teacher be? A man
Among the flatterers in the court
Was found, well-suited to the plan
The tyrant had devised. Report
Gave him a wisdom owned by few,
And certainly to trim his sail,
And veer his bark, none better knew,
Before a changing adverse gale.

And Sonda Marco,—such his name,—
Took home the four fair boys to teach
All knowledge that their years became,
Science, and war, and modes of speech,
But he was told, if death he feared,
Never to tell them of the soul,
Of vows, and prayers, and rites revered,
And of the gods who all control.

The sciences the boys were taught
They mastered with a quickness strange,
But Prehlad was the one for thought,
He soared above the lesson's range.
One day the tutor unseen heard
The boy discuss forbidden themes,
As if his inmost heart were stirred,
And he of truth from heaven had gleams.

"O Prince, what mean'st thou?" In his fright
The teacher thus in private said—
"Talk on such subjects is not right,
Wouldst thou bring ruin on my head?
There are no gods except the king,
The ruler of the world is he!
Look up to him, and do not bring
Destruction by a speech too free."

"Be wary for thy own sake, child,
If he should hear thee talking so,
Thou shalt forever be exiled,
And I shall die, full well I know.
Worthy of worship, honour, praise,
Is thy great father. Things unseen,
What *are* they?—Themes of poets' lays!
They *are* not and have never been."

Smiling, the boy, with folded hands,
As sign of a submission meek,
Answered his tutor. "Thy commands

TORU DUTT

Are ever precious. Do not seek
To lay upon me what I feel
Would be unrighteous. Let me hear
Those inner voices that reveal
Long vistas in another sphere."

"The gods that rule the earth and sea,
 Shall I abjure them and adore
A man? It may not, may not be;
 Though I should lie in pools of gore
My conscience I would hurt no more;
 But I shall follow what my heart
Tells me is right, so I implore
My purpose fixed no longer thwart.

"The coward calls black white, white black,
At bidding, or in fear of death;
 Such suppleness, thank God, I lack,
To die is but to lose my breath.
Is death annihilation? No.
New worlds will open on my view,
When persecuted hence I go,
The right is right,—the true is true."

All's over now, the teacher thought,
 Now let this reach the monarch's ear!
And instant death shall be my lot.
 They parted, he in abject fear.
And soon he heard a choral song
 Sung by young voices in the praise
Of gods unseen, who right all wrong,
And rule the worlds from primal days.

"What progress have thy charges made?
Let them be called, that I may see."
And Sonda Marco brought as bade
 His pupils to the royal knee.
Three passed the monarch's test severe,
 The fourth remained: then spake the king,

"Now, Prehlad, with attention hear,
I know thou hast the strongest wing!"

"What is the cream of knowledge, child,
 Which men take such great pains to learn?"
With folded hands he answered mild:
"Listen, O Sire! To speak I yearn.
All sciences are nothing worth,—
Astronomy that tracks the star,
Geography that maps the earth,
Logic, and Politics, and War,—"

"And Medicine, that strives to heal
 But only aggravates disease,
All, all are futile,—so I feel,
 For me, O father, none of these.
That is true knowledge which can show
The glory of the living gods,—
Divest of pride, make men below
Humble and happy, though but clods.

"That is true knowledge which can make
 Us mortals, saintlike, holy, pure,
The strange thirst of the spirit slake
 And strengthen suffering to endure.
That is true knowledge which can change
Our very natures, with its glow;
The sciences whate'er their range
Feed but the flesh, and make a show."

"Where hast thou learnt this nonsense, boy?
 Where live these gods believed so great?
 Can they like me thy life destroy?
 Have they such troops and royal state?
Above all gods is he who rules
The wide, wide earth, from sea to sea,
Men, devils, gods,—yea, all but fools
Bow down in fear and worship me!

"And dares an atom from my loins
  Against my kingly power rebel?
Though heaven itself to aid him joins,
  His end is death—the infidel!
I warn thee yet,—bow down, thou slave,
  And worship me, or thou shalt die!
We'll see what gods descend to save—
  What gods with me their strength will try!"

Thus spake the monarch in his ire,
  One hand outstretched, in menace rude,
And eyes like blazing coals of fire.
  And Prehlad, in unruffled mood
Straight answered him; his head bent low,
  His palms joined meekly on his breast
As ever, and his cheeks aglow
  His rock-firm purpose to attest.

"Let not my words, Sire, give offence,
  To thee, and to my mother, both
I give as due all reverence,
  And to obey thee am not loth.
But higher duties sometimes clash
  With lower,—then these last must go,—
Or there will come a fearful crash
  In lamentation, fear, and woe!

"The gods who made us are the life
  Of living creatures, small and great;
We see them not, but space is rife
  With their bright presence and their state.
They are the parents of us all,
  'Tis they create, sustain, redeem,
Heaven, earth and hell, they hold in thrall,
  And shall we these high gods blaspheme?

"Blest is the man whose heart obeys
  And makes their law of life his guide,

He shall be led in all his ways,
His footsteps shall not ever slide;
In forests dim, on raging seas,
In certain peace shall he abide,
What though he all the world displease,
His gods shall all his wants provide!"

"Cease, babbler! 'tis enough! I know
Thy proud, rebellious nature well.
Ho! Captain of our lifeguards, ho!
Take down this lad to dungeon-cell,
And bid the executioner wait
Our orders." All unmoved and calm,
He went, as reckless of his fate,
Erect and stately as a palm.

Hushed was the hall, as down he past,
No breath, no whisper, not a sign,
Through ranks of courtiers, all aghast
Like beaten hounds that dare not whine.
Outside the door, the Captain spoke,
"Recant," he said beneath his breath;
"The lion's anger to provoke
Is death, O prince, is certain death."

"Thanks," said the prince,—"I have revolved
The question in my mind with care,
Do what you will,—I am resolved,
To do the right, all deaths I dare.
The gods, perhaps, may please to spare
My tender years; if not,—why, still
I never shall my faith forswear,
I can but say, be done their will."

Whether in pity for the youth,
The headsman would not rightly ply
The weapon, or the gods in truth
Had ordered that he should not die,
Soon to the king there came report

The sword would not destroy his son,
The council held thereon was short,
The king's look frightened everyone.

"There is a spell against cold steel
Which known, the steel can work no harm,
Some sycophant with baneful zeal
Hath taught this foolish boy the charm.
It would be wise, O king, to deal
Someother way, or else I fear
Much damage to the common weal."
Thus spake the wily-tongued vizier.

Dark frowned the king.—"Enough of this,—
Death, instant death, is my command!
Go throw him down some precipice,
Or bury him alive in sand."
With terror dumb, from that wide hall
Departed all the courtier band,
But not one man amongst them all
Dared raise against the prince his hand.

And now vague rumours ran around,
Men talked of them with bated breath:
The river has a depth profound,
The elephants trample down to death,
The poisons kill, the firebrands burn.
Had every means in turn been tried?
Some said they had,—but soon they learn
The brave young prince had not yet died.

For once more in the Council-Hall
He had been cited to appear,
'Twas open to the public all,
And all the people came in fear.
Banners were hung along the wall,
The King sat on his peacock throne,
And now the hoary Marechal
Brings in the youth,—bare skin and bone.

"Who shall protect thee, Prehlad, now?
 Against steel, poison, water, fire,
 Thou art protected, men avow
 Who treason, if but bold, admire.
 In our own presence thou art brought
 That we and all may know the truth—
 Where are thy gods?—I long have sought
 But never found them, hapless youth.

"Will they come down, to prove their strength?
 Will they come down, to rescue thee?
 Let them come down, for once, at length,
 Come one, or all, to fight with me.
 Where are thy gods? Or are they dead,
 Or do they hide in craven fear?
 There lies my gage. None ever said
 I hide from any,—far or near."

"My gracious Liege, my Sire, my King!
 If thou indeed wouldst deign to hear,
 In humble mood, my words would spring
 Like a pellucid fountain clear,
 For I have in my dungeon dark
 Learnt more of truth than e'er I knew,
 There is one God—One only,—mark!
 To Him is all our service due.

"Hath He a shape, or hath He none?
 I know not this, nor care to know,
 Dwelling in light, to which the sun
 Is darkness,—He sees all below,
 Himself unseen! In Him I trust,
 He can protect me if He will,
 And if this body turn to dust,
 He can new life again instil.

"I fear not fire, I fear not sword,
 All dangers, father, I can dare;
 Alone, I can confront a horde,

For oh! my God is everywhere!"
"What! everywhere? Then in this hall,
And in this crystal pillar bright?
Now tell me plain, before us all,
Is He herein, thy God of light?"

The monarch placed his steel-gloved hand
Upon a crystal pillar near,
In mockful jest was his demand,
The answer came, low, serious, clear:
"Yes, father, God is even here,
And if He choose this very hour
Can strike us dead, with ghastly fear,
And vindicate His name and power."

"Where is this God? Now let us see."
He spumed the pillar with his foot,
Down, down it tumbled, like a tree
Severed by axes from the root,
And from within, with horrid clang
That froze the blood in every vein,
A stately sable warrior sprang,
Like some phantasma of the brain.

He had a lion head and eyes,
A human body, feet and hands,
Colossal,—such strange shapes arise
In clouds, when Autumn rules the lands!
He gave a shout;—the boldest quailed,
Then struck the tyrant on the helm,
And ripped him down; and last, he hailed
Prehlad as king of all the realm!

A thunder clap—the shape was gone!
One king lay stiff, and stark, and dead,
Another on the peacock throne
Bowed reverently his youthful head.
Loud rang the trumpets; louder still
A sovereign people's wild acclaim.

The echoes ran from hill to hill,
"Kings rule for us and in our name."

Tyrants of every age and clime
Remember this,—that awful shape
Shall startle you when comes the time,
And send its voice from cape to cape.
As human, peoples suffer pain,
But oh, the lion strength is theirs,
Woe to the king when galls the chain!
Woe, woe, their fury when he dares!

IX

Sîta

Three happy children in a darkened room!
What do they gaze on with wide-open eyes?
A dense, dense forest, where no sunbeam pries,
And in its centre a cleared spot.—There bloom
Gigantic flowers on creepers that embrace
Tall trees; there, in a quiet lucid lake
The white swans glide; there, "whirring from the brake,"
The peacock springs; there, herds of wild deer race;
There, patches gleam with yellow waving grain;
There, blue smoke from strange altars rises light,
There, dwells in peace, the poet-anchorite.
But who is this fair lady? Not in vain
She weeps,—for lo! at every tear she sheds
Tears from three pairs of young eyes fall amain,
And bowed in sorrow are the three young heads.
It is an old, old story, and the lay
Which has evoked sad Sîta from the past
Is by a mother sung. . . 'Tis hushed at last
And melts the picture from their sight away,
Yet shall they dream of it until the day!
When shall those children by their mother's side
Gather, ah me! as erst at eventide?

MISCELLANEOUS POEMS

NEAR HASTINGS

Near Hastings, on the shingle-beach,
 We loitered at the time
When ripens on the wall the peach,
 The autumn's lovely prime.
Far off,—the sea and sky seemed blent,
 The day was wholly done,
The distant town its murmurs sent,
 Strangers,—we were alone.

We wandered slow; sick, weary, faint,
 Then one of us sat down,
No nature hers, to make complaint;—
 The shadows deepened brown.
A lady past,—she was not young,
 But oh! her gentle face
No painter-poet ever sung,
 Or saw such saintlike grace.

She past us,—then she came again,
 Observing at a glance
That we were strangers; one, in pain,—
 Then asked,—Were we from France?
We talked awhile,—some roses red
 That seemed as wet with tears,
She gave my sister, and she said,
 "God bless you both, my dears!"

Sweet were the roses,—sweet and full,
 And large as lotus flowers
That in our own wide tanks we cull
 To deck our Indian bowers.
But sweeter was the love that gave
 Those flowers to one unknown,
I think that He who came to save
 The gift a debt will own.

The lady's name I do not know,
    Her face no more may see,
But yet, oh yet I love her so!
    Blest, happy, may she be!
Her memory will not depart,
    Though grief my years should shade,
Still bloom her roses in my heart!
    And they shall never fade!

FRANCE
1870

Not dead,—oh no,—she cannot die!
    Only a swoon, from loss of blood!
Levite England passes her by,
Help, Samaritan! None is nigh;
    Who shall stanch me this sanguine flood?

Range the brown hair, it blinds her eyne,
    Dash cold water over her face!
Drowned in her blood, she makes no sign,
Give her a draught of generous wine.
    None heed, none hear, to do this grace.

Head of the human column, thus
    Ever in swoon wilt thou remain?
Thought, Freedom, Truth, quenched ominous,
Whence then shall Hope arise for us,
    Plunged in the darkness all again!

No, she stirs!—There's a fire in her glance,
    Ware, oh ware of that broken sword!
What, dare ye for an hour's mischance,
Gather around her, jeering France,
    Attila's own exultant horde?

Lo, she stands up,—stands up e'en now,
    Strong once more for the battle-fray,
Gleams bright the star, that from her brow
Lightens the world. Bow, nations, bow,
    Let her again lead on the way!

The Tree of Life

Broad daylight, with a sense of weariness!
Mine eyes were closed, but I was not asleep,
My hand was in my father's, and I felt
His presence near me. Thus we often past
In silence, hour by hour. What was the need
Of interchanging words when every thought
That in our hearts arose, was known to each,
And every pulse kept time? Suddenly there shone
A strange light, and the scene as sudden changed.
I was awake:—It was an open plain
Illimitable,—stretching, stretching—oh, so far!
And o'er it that strange light,—a glorious light
Like that the stars shed over fields of snow
In a clear, cloudless, frosty winter night,
Only intenser in its brilliance calm.
And in the midst of that vast plain, I saw,
For I was wide awake,—it was no dream,
A tree with spreading branches and with leaves
Of divers kinds,—dead silver and live gold,
Shimmering in radiance that no words may tell!
Beside the tree an Angel stood; he plucked
A few small sprays, and bound them round my head.
Oh, the delicious touch of those strange leaves!
No longer throbbed my brows, no more I felt
The fever in my limbs—"And oh," I cried,
"Bind too my father's forehead with these leaves."
One leaf the Angel took and therewith touched
His forehead, and then gently whispered "Nay!"
Never, oh never had I seen a face
More beautiful than that Angel's, or more full
Of holy pity and of love divine.
Wondering I looked awhile,—then, all at once
Opened my tear-dimmed eyes—When lo! the light
Was gone—the light as of the stars when snow

Lies deep upon the ground. No more, no more,
Was seen the Angel's face. I only found
My father watching patient by my bed,
And holding in his own, close-prest, my hand.

On the Fly-Leaf of Erckmann-Chatrian's novel entitled "Madame Thérèse"

Wavered the foremost soldiers,—then fell back.
Fallen was their leader, and loomed right before
The sullen Prussian cannon, grim and black,
With lighted matches waving. Now, once more,
Patriots and veterans!—Ah! 'Tis in vain!
Back they recoil, though bravest of the brave;
No human troops may stand that murderous rain;
But who is this—that rushes to a grave?

It is a woman,—slender, tall, and brown!
She snatches up the standard as it falls,—
In her hot haste tumbles her dark hair down,
And to the drummer-boy aloud she calls
To beat the charge; then forwards on the *pont*
They dash together;—who could bear to see
A woman and a child, thus Death confront,
Nor burn to follow them to victory?

I read the story and my heart beats fast!
Well might all Europe quail before thee, France,
Battling against oppression! Years have past,
Yet of that time men speak with moistened glance.
Va-nu-pieds! When rose high your Marseillaise
Man knew his rights to earth's remotest bound,
And tyrants trembled. Yours alone the praise!
Ah, had a Washington but then been found!

Sonnet—Baugmaree

A sea of foliage girds our garden round,
　　But not a sea of dull unvaried green,
　　Sharp contrasts of all colours here are seen;
The light-green graceful tamarinds abound
Amid the mangoe clumps of green profound,
　　And palms arise, like pillars gray, between;
　　And o'er the quiet pools the seemuls lean,
Red,—red, and startling like a trumpet's sound.
But nothing can be lovelier than the ranges
　　Of bamboos to the eastward, when the moon
Looks through their gaps, and the white lotus changes
　　Into a cup of silver. One might swoon
　　　　Drunken with beauty then, or gaze and gaze
　　　　On a primeval Eden, in amaze.

Sonnet—The Lotus

Love came to Flora asking for a flower
    That would of flowers be undisputed queen,
    The lily and the rose, long, long had been
Rivals for that high honour. Bards of power
Had sung their claims. "The rose can never tower
    Like the pale lily with her Juno mien"—
    "But is the lily lovelier?" Thus between
Flower-factions rang the strife in Psyche's bower.
"Give me a flower delicious as the rose
    And stately as the lily in her pride"—
"But of what colour?"—"Rose-red," Love first chose,
    Then prayed,—"No, lily-white,—or, both provide";
    And Flora gave the lotus, "rose-red" dyed,
And "lily-white,"—the queenliest flower that blows.

Our Casuarina Tree

Like a huge Python, winding round and round
    The rugged trunk, indented deep with scars
    Up to its very summit near the stars,
A creeper climbs, in whose embraces bound
    No other tree could live. But gallantly
The giant wears the scarf, and flowers are hung
In crimson clusters all the boughs among,
    Whereon all day are gathered bird and bee;
And oft at nights the garden overflows
With one sweet song that seems to have no close,
Sung darkling from our tree, while men repose.

When first my casement is wide open thrown
    At dawn, my eyes delighted on it rest;
    Sometimes, and most in winter,—on its crest
A grey baboon sits statue-like alone
    Watching the sunrise; while on lower boughs
His puny offspring leap about and play;
And far and near kokilas hail the day;
    And to their pastures wend our sleepy cows;
And in the shadow, on the broad tank cast
By that hoar tree, so beautiful and vast,
The water-lilies spring, like snow enmassed.

But not because of its magnificence
    Dear is the Casuarina to my soul:
    Beneath it we have played; though years may roll,
O sweet companions, loved with love intense,
    For your sakes, shall the tree be ever dear!
Blent with your images, it shall arise
In memory, till the hot tears blind mine eyes!
    What is that dirge-like murmur that I hear
Like the sea breaking on a shingle-beach?
It is the tree's lament, an eerie speech,
That haply to the unknown land may reach.

Unknown, yet well-known to the eye of faith!
    Ah, I have heard that wail far, far away
    In distant lands, by many a sheltered bay,
When slumbered in his cave the water-wraith
    And the waves gently kissed the classic shore
Of France or Italy, beneath the moon,
When earth lay trancèd in a dreamless swoon:
    And everytime the music rose,—before
Mine inner vision rose a form sublime,
Thy form, O Tree, as in my happy prime
I saw thee, in my own loved native clime.

Therefore I fain would consecrate a lay
    Unto thy honour, Tree, beloved of those
    Who now in blessed sleep, for aye, repose,
Dearer than life to me, alas! were they!
    Mayst thou be numbered when my days are done
With deathless trees—like those in Borrowdale,
Under whose awful branches lingered pale
    "Fear, trembling Hope, and Death, the skeleton,
And Time the shadow"; and though weak the verse
That would thy beauty fain, oh fain rehearse,
May Love defend thee from Oblivion's curse.

A Note About the Author

Toru Dutt (1856–1877) was a Bengali poet and translator. Born in Calcutta to a prominent family of Bengali Christians, Dutt was educated from a young age and became a devoted student of English literature. Taught by her father and a private tutor, she learned French, Sanskrit, and English in addition to her native Bengali. At thirteen, she left India with her family to travel through Europe, visiting France, England, Italy, and Germany over the next several years. In 1872, she attended a series of lectures for women at the University of Cambridge alongside her sister Aru, which further sparked her interest in academia and literature. In 1873, the family returned to Calcutta, where Dutt struggled to readjust to Indian culture. She wrote two novels in English and French before publishing *A Sheaf Gleaned in French Fields* (1876), a collection of French poems translated into English. Its critical and commercial success came tragically late, however, as Dutt died of consumption in 1877 at the age of 21. She has since been recognized as the first Indian writer to publish a novel in French, the first Indian woman to publish an English novel, and a pioneering figure in Anglo-Indian literature whose mastery of several languages at such a young age remains remarkably uncommon. *Ancient Ballads and Legends of Hindustan* (1882), a collection of Sanskrit poems translated into English, was her final, posthumously published work.

A Note from the Publisher

Spanning many genres, from non-fiction essays to literature classics to children's books and lyric poetry, Mint Edition books showcase the master works of our time in a modern new package. The text is freshly typeset, is clean and easy to read, and features a new note about the author in each volume. Many books also include exclusive new introductory material. Every book boasts a striking new cover, which makes it as appropriate for collecting as it is for gift giving. Mint Edition books are only printed when a reader orders them, so natural resources are not wasted. We're proud that our books are never manufactured in excess and exist only in the exact quantity they need to be read and enjoyed.

Discover more of your favorite classics with Bookfinity™.

- Track your reading with custom book lists.
- Get great book recommendations for your personalized Reader Type.
- Add reviews for your favorite books.
- AND MUCH MORE!

Visit **bookfinity.com** and take the fun Reader Type quiz to get started.

Enjoy our classic and modern companion pairings!